Development of the Industrial United States (1870-1900)

★★ **PRESIDENTS OF THE UNITED STATES** ★★

By Tom Robinson

WEIGL PUBLISHERS INC.

Published by Weigl Publishers Inc.
350 5th Avenue, Suite 3304 PMB 6G
New York, NY 10118-0069
Website: www.weigl.com

        Library of Congress Cataloging-in-Publication Data

Robinson, Tom, 1964-
   The development of the industrial United States / Tom Robinson.
      p. cm. -- (Presidents of the United States)
   Includes bibliographical references and index.
   ISBN 978-1-59036-745-2 (hard cover : alk. paper) -- ISBN 978-1-59036-746-9 (soft cover : alk. paper)
   1. Presidents--United States--Biography--Juvenile literature. 2. Presidents--United States--History--19th century--Juvenile literature. 3. United States--History--1865-1898--Juvenile literature. 4. United States--Politics and government--1865-1900--Juvenile literature. 5. Industrialization--United States--History--19th century--Juvenile literature. 6. United States--Economic conditions--1865-1918--Juvenile literature. I. Title.
   E176.1.R645 2008
   973'.09'9--dc22
   [B]
                              2007012646

Printed in the United States of America
1 2 3 4 5 6 7 8 9 0 11 10 09 08 07

Project Coordinator
Heather C. Hudak

Design
Terry Paulhus

Photo Credits
Every reasonable effort has been made to trace ownership and to obtain permission to reprint copyright material. The publishers would be pleased to have any errors or omissions brought to their attention so that they may be corrected in subsequent printings.

All of the Internet URLs given in the book were valid at the time of publication. However, due to the dynamic nature of the Internet, some addresses may have changed, or sites may have ceased to exist since publication. While the author and publisher regret any inconvenience this may cause readers, no responsibility for any such changes can be accepted by either the author or the publisher.

Contents

United States Presidents

REVOLUTION AND THE NEW NATION (1750–EARLY 1800s)

George Washington
(1789–1797)

John Adams
(1797–1801)

Thomas Jefferson
(1801–1809)

James Madison
(1809–1817)

James Monroe
(1817–1825)

EXPANSION AND REFORM (EARLY 1800s–1861)

John Quincy Adams
(1825–1829)

Andrew Jackson
(1829–1837)

Martin Van Buren
(1837–1841)

William Henry Harrison
(1841)

John Tyler
(1841–1845)

James Polk
(1845–1849)

Zachary Taylor
(1849–1850)

Millard Fillmore
(1850–1853)

Franklin Pierce
(1853–1857)

James Buchanan
(1857–1861)

CIVIL WAR AND RECONSTRUCTION (1850–1877)

Abraham Lincoln
(1861–1865)

Andrew Johnson
(1865–1869)

Ulysses S. Grant
(1869–1877)

DEVELOPMENT OF THE INDUSTRIAL UNITED STATES (1870–1900)

Rutherford B. Hayes
(1877–1881)

James Garfield
(1881)

Chester Arthur
(1881–1885)

Grover Cleveland
(1885–1889)
(1893–1897)

Benjamin Harrison
(1889–1893)

William McKinley
(1897–1901)

THE EMERGENCE OF MODERN AMERICA (1890–1930)

 Theodore Roosevelt
(1901–1909)

 William H. Taft
(1909–1913)

 Woodrow Wilson
(1913–1921)

 Warren Harding
(1921–1923)

 Calvin Coolidge
(1923–1929)

THE GREAT DEPRESSION AND WORLD WAR II (1929–1945)

 Herbert Hoover
(1929–1933)

 Franklin D. Roosevelt
(1933–1945)

POST-WAR UNITED STATES (1945–EARLY 1970s)

 Harry S. Truman
(1945–1953)

 Dwight Eisenhower
(1953–1961)

 John F. Kennedy
(1961–1963)

 Lyndon Johnson
(1963–1969)

CONTEMPORARY UNITED STATES (1968 TO THE PRESENT)

 Richard Nixon
(1969–1974)

 Gerald Ford
(1974–1977)

 Jimmy Carter
(1977–1981)

 Ronald Reagan
(1981–1989)

 George H. W. Bush
(1989–1993)

 William J. Clinton
(1993–2001)

 George W. Bush
(2001–)

The Development of the Industrial United States

Thomas Edison was a well-known American inventor. Edison invented the lightbulb and the phonograph.

The Civil War that divided the United States was over. Reconstruction, the rebuilding of the Southern states, was drawing to an end. Once the enormous task of recovering from the Civil War was overcome, the United States embarked on an era of growth. In the period from 1870 to 1900, the United States became an industrialized nation.

Georgia, Virginia, Mississippi, and Texas were readmitted as states in 1870. Resentment between the North and the South was slowly overcome. The nation was rebuilt as each of the former Confederate states agreed to terms of the 14th Amendment, which established post-war changes in the nation.

As the country moved forward, technological innovations inspired big business and altered the way farming was done. Alexander Graham Bell invented the telephone in 1876, and Thomas Edison invented the light bulb in 1879. Other inventions helped the United States become the world's largest food producer.

With growth, there were challenges. Labor unions organized, and major conflicts developed between workers and business owners.

The nation was in transition in other ways as well. The population was growing, in part through immigration. The population was shifting, as the pioneer spirit continued to move people to the West, where they settled on previously undeveloped land.

The presidents of the industrial era concentrated on ending political favoritism. The Civil Service Commission was created in an attempt to assure that government jobs went to the most qualified people rather than being considered repayment for political favors.

The women's movement was growing. Women were finally allowed to practice law in front of the U.S. Supreme Court. Women began their push to vote.

As the 20th century approached, development of the industrial United States was complete. By this time, the country was taking on a stronger global presence. The Spanish-American War developed, in part, from the United States protecting the human rights of citizens of Spanish colonies.

The debates that led up to and followed the Spanish-American War made it clear that the United States had other interests. By gaining control over these territories, the United States expanded its reach. The addition of Hawai'i, which became a state, and the control of the Philippines and Guam as territories, expanded the United States' reach into the Pacific Ocean. This made the United States better able to protect itself from potential enemies in Asia.

The Philippines, Guam, and Puerto Rico were all added to the United States as part of the Treaty of Paris following the Spanish-American War. These added territories and the way U.S. forces soundly defeated Spain in the war established the United States as a growing international power.

Rutherford B. Hayes' Early Years and Early Political Career

Rutherford B. Hayes had a difficult start in life. Hayes was born October 4, 1822, 11 weeks after the death of his father. Young "Rud," who was named after his late father, was a sickly infant. His mother, Sophia Birchard Hayes, who had already lost one child, was now raising three children on her own. Just when 2-year-old Rutherford's health began improving, the family was struck by tragedy again. Hayes' 9-year-old brother drowned by falling through the ice while skating.

Rutherford's family had moved from Dummerston, Vermont, to Delaware, Ohio, five years before he was born. Sophia's brother, Sardis Birchard, settled in Lower Sandusky, Ohio. Uncle Sardis tried to help look after Rutherford and his sister, Fanny. With the help of sharecroppers who worked the land, Sophia ran the Hayes farm and took care of her family.

Fanny was a bright student. She helped teach her younger brother about plays and poetry. Uncle Sardis made sure the

Rutherford B. Hayes began his political career before the Civil War broke out.

Hayes served as a Union general during the Civil War.

children could attend private schools. Rutherford went on to become valedictorian of the class of 1842 at Kenyon College in Gambier, Ohio. His success as a student led to Rutherford earning a law degree from Harvard and passing the Ohio bar exam in 1845. He opened a law practice in Lower Sandusky, which was renamed Fremont.

Hayes moved to Cincinnati and became a criminal lawyer. While there, he met Lucy Webb, a girl from his hometown who attended Cincinnati Wesleyan Women's College. The couple was engaged in 1851 and married a year later. They had eight children, but only five of them lived to be adults.

Hayes' political career began in 1858, as the attorney for the Cincinnati City Council. When the Civil War broke out in 1861, Hayes left his career and his family to enlist. At the time, Lucy was pregnant with their fourth child.

Political supporters nominated Hayes for a seat in the U.S. House of Representatives in July, 1864, but he refused to come home to campaign. Two months later, Hayes suffered one of his four war wounds. The press even reported, incorrectly, that he had been killed in action.

When Hayes refused to come home, his actions added to his popularity. He was elected to the 39th Congress while still at war. One year after being re-elected to the House of Representatives, Hayes resigned to run for governor of Ohio. He served two terms as governor before running for Congress while supporting the presidential campaign of Ulysses S. Grant. He lost the election.

Hayes' Presidency

Ohio Republicans convinced Hayes to run for governor again after he was defeated in his bid for Congress. He won a third term as governor in 1875.

Hayes was serving as governor of Ohio when the Republican National Convention came to Cincinnati in 1876. The convention was held to determine the party's **nominee** for president. The leading candidates were unable to gain a majority. By the time a fifth vote was held, Hayes was gaining support to be the Republican nominee. In the seventh vote, Hayes had the majority and became the party's nominee.

Hayes barely defeated New York governor Samuel Jones Tilden in a controversial presidential race. Tilden received almost 250,000 more votes. Hayes, however, ultimately had an edge in **electoral college** votes, 185-184, after the commission sorted out disputed races in Florida, Louisiana, and South Carolina.

Some historians believe that a compromise was reached behind closed doors to bring an end to the election dispute in 1876. Historian C. Vann Woodward called it the "Compromise of 1877."

According to the theory, the election dispute ended when Hayes or his representatives agreed to some terms. Those terms included the removal of federal troops from statehouse property in South Carolina and Louisiana, the commitment of funds to build the Texas and Pacific Railroad, the appointment of a southerner to the president's Cabinet, and other commitments to aid the Southern economy.

> **"He serves his party best who serves his country best."**
> *Rutherford B. Hayes,*
> *Inaugural Address, 1877*

Hayes became president in 1877 after a close and controversial election.

Hayes had pressing issues to face early in his presidency. The Desert Land Act passed in 1877, allowed for the inexpensive purchase of undeveloped government land. To get the land, the new owner had to irrigate, or water, the land. Members of the Brotherhood of Locomotive Engineers walked off their jobs in Martinsburg, West Virginia, in 1877, triggering a series of railroad strikes to protest cuts in wages. The railroad strikes were just one sign of an economy still struggling to recover from the damage done during the Civil War.

During the war, the U.S. Treasury had issued millions of "**greenbacks**." The greenbacks were not backed by gold, meaning the treasury did not have the actual gold to give people if they wanted to turn them in. The government promised to buy enough gold to back the greenbacks by January 1, 1879. When that plan could not be honored, Congress had enough support to override a **veto** by Hayes and passed the Bland-Allison Bill calling for a system of silver coinage.

ELECTORAL COLLEGE

Rutherford B. Hayes is the only U.S. president to have his election decided by a congressional commission.

Votes from the electoral college, not actual votes from the public, determine the president. The electoral college is a body of electors chosen from each state. The number of electors is equal to the number of senators and representatives from the state. In all states but Maine, the candidate that receives the most votes in the state receives all of that state's electoral votes.

Some railroads were destroyed during the strikes in 1877.

Hayes' Legacy

Hayes followed the scandal-plagued presidency of Ulysses S. Grant and came into office following a disputed election. During his campaign and inauguration, Hayes pledged to only serve one term. This way he would prove that he would not be obligated to return political favors.

Hayes stuck to his one-term promise and handled many other delicate situations to restore prestige to the office of president. Hayes developed a reputation for appointing the most qualified individuals, rather than those he owed favors to. He balanced protecting the constitutional rights of all citizens with eliminating federal interference in local government in Southern states.

> **"I am a radical in thought and a conservative in method."**
> *Rutherford B. Hayes*

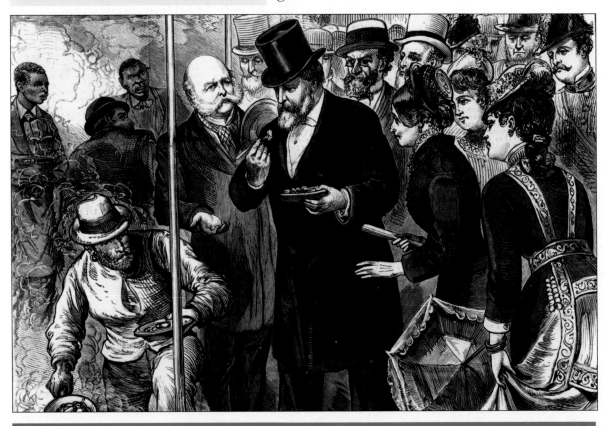

President Hayes visited Rhode Island during his presidency.

During his presidency, Hayes addressed issues to try to stabilize the nation's long-term economy. He attempted to continue the country's recovery from the Civil War. He made changes where he could but compromised to try to make peace.

Hayes' legacy included signing a bill that allowed female attorneys to appear before the U.S. Supreme Court for the first time. In an era when Congress had established its power over the president, Hayes traveled and spoke to the public often. By speaking about issues and explaining his actions, he effectively went to the people for support.

When Hayes upheld his decision not to run again for president, he had strengthened his party to the point that James Garfield, another Republican from Ohio, was able to win the presidency.

In retirement, Hayes returned to Spiegel Grove, the beautiful, Fremont, Ohio, home he inherited from his Uncle Sardis. Hayes avoided most political issues in his retirement years, but did continue working to reform the prison system. He raised money to provide educational opportunities, particularly for African Americans in the South.

Hayes lost Lucy, his wife of 36 years, to a stroke in 1889. He passed away from heart failure at his home on January 17, 1893. He is buried, along with his family, at Spiegel Grove, which is now part of the Rutherford B. Hayes Presidential Center.

Hayes kept his promise to serve only one term as president.

Women in the Supreme Court

The 19th Amendment to the U.S. Constitution, giving women the right to vote, was not **ratified** until August 26, 1920. Women, however, were gaining momentum toward their goal prior to and during the development of the industrial United States. Women gained the right to argue cases as attorneys in front of the U.S. Supreme Court under president Rutherford B. Hayes. This was nearly a half century before they were allowed to vote.

Lucy Hayes, wife of President Hayes, had political interests that were similar to many of the leaders of the women's rights movement. Lucy Hayes was an advocate of **prohibition**, or the outlawing of alcohol, during her husband's presidency. The largest organization in the United States backing the cause was the Woman's Christian **Temperance** Union, which formed in 1874. Many of the same women who worked for voting rights were involved in the push that led to alcohol being prohibited in the United States from 1920 to 1933.

The National Woman **Suffrage** Association was formed in 1869. This group advocated women's suffrage. Suffrage is the right to vote. Women still struggled to obtain equal rights in many other areas as well.

Belva Lockwood completed her law courses at the National University of Law School in Washington, D.C., in 1873. She

President Hayes' wife, Lucy, like many other women of her time, was an advocate of prohibition.

was refused her diploma until she demanded it from President Ulysses S. Grant. Once admitted to the Washington, D.C., bar, Lockwood began specializing in cases against the government. In 1874, she was denied permission to argue before the U.S. Court of Claims because she was a woman.

President Hayes backed a bill allowing women to practice law before the Supreme Court. The bill passed both houses of Congress, and Hayes signed it into law in 1879.

Lockwood became the first woman to practice law before the Supreme Court. Even though women were still not allowed to vote, Lockwood received 4,149 votes for president when she ran for the office in 1884.

The pursuit of women's rights remained a prominent part of Lockwood's career. She took cases seeking equal guardianship of children and equal property rights. She continued to promote women's rights and temperance.

Lockwood's determination to practice law before the Supreme Court paved the way for other women in the judicial field. In 1981, President Ronald Reagan appointed Sandra Day O'Connor to be the first female Supreme Court Justice.

> **"For the first time in my life I began to realize it's a crime to be a woman, but it's too late to put in a denial so I pled guilty."**
> *Belva Lockwood*

Belva Lockwood was a lawyer and women's rights advocate. She was the first woman to practice law in front of the Supreme Court.

James Garfield's Early Years and Early Political Career

James Garfield emerged from humble beginnings to become president of the United States. He was born on November 19, 1831. James' father, Abram, died when James was two years old. Two of Abram and Eliza Garfield's other children had also passed away. James grew up on a farm in Cuyahoga County, Ohio.

> "I am inclined to believe that the sin of slavery is one of which it may be said that without the shedding of blood there is no remission."
> *James Garfield, 1860*

Garfield served as a part-time teacher, carpenter, and janitor to work his way through school. He graduated from Williams College in Massachusetts in 1856, at the age of 24. He returned to teach at one of his earlier schools, Geauga Academy in Chester, Ohio. He quickly earned a promotion to president of the school. While working at Geauga, Garfield married Lucretia "Crete" Rudolph and studied law.

Garfield and his wife, Lucretia, had seven children, but two of them died as infants.

Garfield, who had campaigned for Abraham Lincoln during the 1860 presidential election, joined the military and organized the 42nd Ohio Infantry. Garfield rose through the military ranks with the Union during the Civil War. By 1863, he was the youngest officer to hold the rank of major general. Much like Rutherford B. Hayes, Garfield's status as a war hero won him an election for which he had never campaigned.

After the citizens of Ohio elected Garfield to Congress, he resigned his military commission. He began 18 years of service in the U.S. House of Representatives. Garfield won re-election eight times and developed a reputation for a strong understanding of financial issues. He was chairman of the Banking and Currency Committee. Garfield was one of the Republicans who served on the 15-member committee that resolved the election dispute of 1876, declaring Hayes the winner by one electoral vote.

Garfield became a nominee for president in 1880 on the 36th ballot at the Republican convention. The party chose him over James G. Blaine and former president Ulysses S. Grant. The Democrats nominated Winfield S. Hancock, a Civil War hero. Hancock had been one of the prominent figures at Gettysburg, one of the most famous Civil War battles. Neither candidate managed to receive the majority, and less than one-tenth of one percent—just 7,368 votes—separated them. Garfield, however, won the key states and had a much larger edge in the electoral college, 214 to 155.

Garfield and his running mate, Chester Arthur, were successful in their campaign. They were elected as president and vice president in 1880.

Garfield's Assassination and Legacy

Garfield continued progress in areas where President Rutherford B. Hayes had started making changes. He worked against **patronage**, the process of distributing jobs and favors on a political basis. Garfield called for African-American suffrage during his inaugural address and furthered the educational cause of African Americans.

Garfield set out to work on foreign affairs by inviting Latin American countries to a conference in Washington, D.C., in 1882. The conference never happened. His presidency was cut short when he was shot by an assassin less than four months after taking office. Garfield was shot on July 2, 1881, by Charles Julius Guiteau, a man who had sought a position in his administration. Alexander Graham Bell, the inventor of the telephone, used an electrical device to attempt to locate the bullet that was trapped in Garfield's body. The president was moved to the New Jersey shore from Washington, D. C., on September 6, and he briefly appeared to be making progress toward recovery.

Charles Julius Guiteau shot President Garfield in the back while the president was on his way to the train station. Doctors were unable to remove the bullet, and Garfield died from blood poisoning.

Infection set in, and heavy bleeding developed. Garfield passed away on September 19.

The president was survived by his wife, Lucretia Garfield, who lived to be almost 86, and five of their children.

Although his presidency was short, Garfield's legacy is one of civil service reform. Garfield withstood bitter debates with powerful New York Senator Roscoe Conkling to strengthen Federal authority over the New York Custom House. Conkling was a Stalwart Republican, meaning he believed in patronage. The Customs House had long been a source of the most profitable forms of patronage. When Garfield would not back down and withdrew some nominations that Conkling favored, Conkling resigned.

When he formed his cabinet, Garfield made a point of breaking from those who might be influenced by the power of eastern bankers. His appointments included Robert T. Lincoln, the son of Abraham Lincoln, as his secretary of war.

> **"Next in importance to freedom and justice is education, without which neither freedom nor justice can be permanently maintained."**
> *James Garfield*

Garfield died two and half months after he was shot.

Chester Arthur's Early Years and Early Political Career

Chester Arthur was born October 5, 1829 in Fairfield, Vermont to William and Malvina Arthur. William Arthur was a Baptist Minister. He moved his family often from one parish to another on each side of the Vermont-New York border. When Chester was 10, the family settled in Union Village, New York.

The Arthur family moved to Schenectady, New York, about four years later. Prior to his 16th birthday, Arthur enrolled as a sophomore at Union College. He was active in the school's debating society and wrote for the school newspaper.

Chester Arthur was the 21st president of the United States.

Arthur taught school during and after his college years and continued to study. He became a lawyer, passing the bar exam in 1854. Arthur moved to New York City to work for the law firm headed by **abolitionist** Erastus D. Culver. Arthur's father had been active in politics, with strong abolitionist stances. Arthur made several political connections of his own by working on two prominent cases involving African Americans.

Arthur began attending Republican meetings and working on campaigns. He joined the state militia and became quartermaster general of the New York Volunteers, a high-level administrative position. Arthur built his reputation for being efficient and organized. Arthur never saw combat duty during the Civil War, which probably saved him from problems with his family. With his new wife Ellen "Nell" Lewis Herndon, from Virginia, and a sister who had married a man from Virginia, Arthur had family connections to the South.

Arthur was chairman of the state Republican executive committee in 1868. He was appointed to a position as Collector of the Port of New York in 1871 in a move that was seen as an example of the patronage that was common at the time. When Rutherford B. Hayes became president in 1877, he asked Arthur to resign his position with the New York Custom House.

Although James Garfield followed Hayes in working to eliminate political favors, he chose Arthur to be his vice presidential running mate. Garfield needed support from New York to carry the election. He seemed to believe that Arthur was not just well connected, but also an effective politician.

Garfield won the election but was shot four months later, putting Arthur in a position where he would ultimately take over as president upon Garfield's death.

Arthur was at home in New York City when he learned of Garfield's death. He was sworn in as the 21st president on September 20, 1881.

Arthur campaigned for the 1880 election in upstate New York.

Arthur's Presidency and Legacy

Arthur was hurt by the assassin's implication that the shooting would benefit Arthur's political career. He resisted suggestions that he should officially assume the presidency before Garfield died.

Arthur entered office a year after the death of his wife, Nell. The couple had two children, Chester Alan II and Ellen. President Arthur's younger sister, Mary Arthur McElroy, served as his official hostess while he was in office.

There was some skepticism when Arthur became president. There were concerns that he would return to the old Stalwart ways. Many people believed he would hand out the political favors that presidents Hayes and Garfield had sought to eliminate. Arthur, however, followed the principles set by Garfield. He asked all of Garfield's Cabinet members to stay through December and promised he would not appoint Stalwarts to profitable positions with the New York Custom House. When changes were made to the cabinet, Arthur went with a combination of Stalwarts and moderates.

Along with vowing that federal appointments would be made on basis of ability, Arthur stated that complaints of political hiring should be investigated immediately.

Arthur carried out Garfield's plans for civil service reform. At Arthur's urging, Congress established the Civil Service Commission when it passed the Pendleton Civil Service

> **"I did it and will go to jail for it. I am a Stalwart and Arthur will be President."**
> *Charles Julius Guiteau, after shooting James Garfield*

Arthur became president when James Garfield was assassinated in 1881.

Reform Act in January 1883. Applicants for civil service jobs were chosen based on tests. The act prohibited firing for political reasons and eliminated "voluntary contributions." These voluntary contributions were often payments from public employees to the political parties that arranged their hiring.

When Arthur ordered the U.S. attorney general to prosecute fraud cases within the Post Office Department, many of his friends and associates were found guilty. Support for Arthur weakened, and the Republican Party was divided.

Arthur vetoed a bill that would eliminate almost all immigration from China for 20 years. President Hayes had negotiated with China in 1880 to place limits on the number of immigrants that would be allowed. When Congress sought to pass the Chinese Exclusion Act of 1882, Arthur blocked it. He believed it violated the Burlingame Treaty of 1868 that Hayes had signed. Congress revised the bill and reached a compromise with Arthur.

Battling a serious kidney disease, Arthur did not seek re-election in 1884. He died at home in New York City on November 18, 1886. Arthur was buried in the family plot in Albany, New York.

> **"Honors to me now are not what they once were."**
> *Chester Arthur, on rising to the presidency after the death of his wife, Nell.*

Arthur did not seek re-election because of illness.

Grover Cleveland's Early Years and Early Political Career

Grover Cleveland was born March 18, 1837, in Caldwell, New Jersey. He was the fifth of nine children. Cleveland grew up in Fayetteville and Clinton, New York, where his father, Stephen Grover Cleveland, was a Presbyterian minister. With his father ill, Grover left school and went to work to help support the family. His father died when Grover was 16.

> "Honor lies in honest toil."
> *Grover Cleveland*

Grover Cleveland and his wife, Frances, had five children.

Cleveland served as governor of New York from 1882 to 1884.

Cleveland began working in a law office when he was 18. Without even having attended law school, he was admitted to the New York State bar when he was 22. Cleveland got his start in politics when he worked on the campaign of Democrat James Buchanan in 1856. Cleveland was drafted into the Civil War, but took advantage of a legal option at the time and paid someone to take his place. If he went to war, there would be no one to help support his mother and sisters. By 1863, Cleveland was the assistant district attorney for Erie County, New York.

Cleveland became sheriff of Erie County in 1871. He was a surprise winner for mayor of Buffalo in 1881. As mayor, Cleveland built a reputation by exposing corruption in the city municipal departments. These departments managed street cleaning, sewage, and transportation. He helped to cut the city's budget by vetoing, or rejecting, several expensive measures passed by the city council.

The Democratic Party noticed his work and nominated Cleveland for governor of New York. Cleveland won and led the state from 1882 to 1884. Cleveland continued to fight against waste in government.

Cleveland even challenged Tammany Hall, a New York City-based organization that had powerful political influence. Tammany Hall benefitted greatly from patronage, a practice that Cleveland saw as being corrupt. His interference with Tammany Hall angered some in his party, but he gained support from many other Democrats and concerned citizens. Party leaders around the nation were seeing Cleveland as the type of reformer who could bring a Democrat back to the White House for the first time since the Civil War.

Cleveland's Presidency

President James Buchanan, the man Cleveland had campaigned for in 1856, was the last successful Democratic candidate to run for president until Cleveland. Cleveland emerged as a Democratic presidential candidate in 1884.

Cleveland's campaign focused on running an honest and efficient government. His record as mayor and governor backed his claims.

Controlling New York made the difference for Cleveland in a close election. He had an advantage of just three-tenths of a percent, or 29,214 votes out of nearly 10 million. A close win in New York state gave Cleveland a 219 to 182 victory in electoral votes.

As president, Cleveland supported a bill to establish the Interstate Commerce Commission and, in February 1887, he signed the Interstate Commerce Act into law. The act gave the government the ability to regulate business practices that affected fair commerce and the public. Prior to the act, railroads had the right to charge whatever amount they wanted. Railroads often charged farmers more to ship their crops than they charged mines to ship coal and iron. The fees were threatening the profitability of the entire farming industry.

> **"What is the use of being elected or re-elected unless you stand for something?"**
> *Grover Cleveland, on refusing to change his position on tariffs*

Crowds of people in New York City celebrated the inauguration of Grover Cleveland.

Cleveland signed the Dawes Act of 1887 into law. Although he had not campaigned for it, he supported the Dawes Act, which empowered the president to allot land within reservations to individual American Indians. The surplus land would revert to the public domain. The act took away much of the remaining land that belonged to American Indians and did little to improve their way of life.

When it came time to run for re-election in 1888, one of Cleveland's clear policies was a reduction on **tariffs**. A tariff is a tax charged on an **import** or **export**. His Republican opponent, Benjamin Harrison, was a supporter of tariffs. The tariff issue helped Harrison win New York state and its electoral votes. Although Cleveland won the popular vote, 48.6 to 47.9 percent, Harrison took the states with the most electoral votes and won the presidency.

Cleveland served as president from 1885 to 1889.

FRANCES CLEVELAND

Grover Cleveland was the only president to get married in the White House and the first to have a child born while there.

Prior to becoming mayor of Buffalo, Cleveland had gone into law practice with Oscar Folsam. When Folsam died, Cleveland was the administrator of his estate, helping to look after Folsam's wife and young daughter, Frances.

Frances, known to many as "Frankie," would later become the First Lady. She was 21 and a recent college graduate when she married the 49-year-old president on June 2, 1886. Frances was young, charming, and pretty. Women copied her clothing and hairstyles. She was so popular, her face was used to sell many kinds of products. She gave receptions weekly, one being on Saturday so working women could attend. She championed other women's causes, such as temperance of alcohol and women's education.

Cleveland's Second Term and Legacy

Cleveland was the only president to serve non-consecutive terms. He left office after losing the election in 1888, but he won the election of 1892 and returned for a second term. The leadership of the Republican Party was in disarray, and much of the country battled economic hardship. This allowed Cleveland to easily win the 1892 election.

By the time Cleveland took office again, the nation was entering the most severe **economic depression** it had ever faced. Unemployment levels reached 18 percent in 1894. Railroad construction slowed, cutting the market for rails and hurting the steel industry. About 10 percent of banks shut down. Charities could not provide for the large number of people who were hungry and needed clothing and shelter.

A parade in Chicago celebrated Cleveland's second term.

Cleveland blamed the Sherman Silver Purchase Act of 1890 for the economic problems. The act, passed during Harrison's presidency, required the U.S. Treasury to purchase 4.5 million ounces of silver a month to be coined as silver dollars. Cleveland always supported a system in which all paper money would be backed by gold. He believed that inflating the money supply undermined confidence in the value of American dollars. It also punished banks and other creditors by paying them back dollars that were less valuable than what they had originally loaned.

The McKinley Tariff Act, a Republican legislation that was passed in 1890, was controversial. This legislation created large protective tariffs. It was blamed for higher prices and wage cuts.

Cleveland succeeded in getting the Sherman Silver Purchase Act repealed, but it cost him the support of many in his party. It did not solve the country's financial woes. Instead, the United States struggled to replenish its gold reserves.

> **"I have tried so hard to do right."**
> *Grover Cleveland's final words*

Beyond the financial issues and struggles, Cleveland built a legacy as the "guardian president." Although he did not believe in proposing legislation, he used his veto power more than any president who had come before him. By using this power against Congress, Cleveland strengthened the executive branch of government.

Unlike other presidents in the years following the Civil War, Cleveland did not improve the treatment of African Americans. He tried to keep government out of race and social issues. In doing so, he became popular among southerners with roots to the Confederacy. Cleveland took actions that hurt the cause of the American Indians by taking away their land.

Cleveland was regarded as an honest and independent president. Rather than leading and pursuing an agenda, however, he was more likely to appoint qualified cabinet members and ask for their advice.

Following his presidency, Cleveland settled in Princeton, New Jersey, where he resumed his law practice. Cleveland died in Princeton on June 24, 1908.

Grover Cleveland is the only president to serve non-consecutive terms.

The Pullman Strike

"If it takes the entire army and navy of the United States to deliver a postal card in Chicago, that card will be delivered."

Grover Cleveland

The nation was struggling with an economic depression in 1893. The stock market crashed on June 27. It was not long before the impact of the crash was felt by the Pullman Company, which made railroad sleeper cars.

George Pullman, president of the company, had built the town of Pullman, Illinois, around his business. The company town worked without major problems for more than a decade. Workers all lived in the same town, did their banking at the Pullman bank, and had their rent deducted from weekly paychecks from the company.

With orders for new railroad cars declining and business suffering, Pullman began laying off workers and cut the pay of others. Rent deductions, however, remained the same. Workers had less money to feed and clothe their families.

Employees became fed up with not having enough money. They demanded lower rents and higher pay. When the demands were not met, they walked off their jobs.

Eugene V. Debs and the American Railway Union came to the defense of the Pullman workers. Debs, a longtime railroad worker and politician, had created the American Railway Union to represent railroad workers. Across the country, railroad workers began boycotting trains carrying Pullman cars. Rioting ensued, and railroad cars were set on fire.

George Pullman was the president of Pullman Company.

Mail service was interrupted, and executives of other railroad companies were becoming uneasy. President Grover Cleveland declared the strike a national crime. He deployed 12,000 troops to break the strike. Two men were killed when U.S. deputy marshals fired on protesters in Kensington, Illinois, near Chicago.

Pullman employees gave in on August 3, 1894. The American Railway Union disbanded, and Debs was sent to prison. Pullman employees pledged that they would never again try to form a union.

Reaction to the way Cleveland ended the Pullman Strike left him in need of a way to appease the nation's workforce. Prior to the Pullman Strike, workers had been pushing for Labor Day as a national holiday. Union workers in New York City had taken an unpaid day off in September 1892, to march around the city in support of the holiday. Legislation was drafted and rushed through both houses of Congress, passing unanimously. Just six days after the Pullman Strike came to an end, Labor Day was declared as the nation's newest holiday.

U.S. troops were called in to protect railroads during the Pullman Strike.

Benjamin Harrison's Early Years and Early Political Career

Benjamin Harrison was born on August 20, 1833, in North Bend, Ohio. He was born into a prominent family with a lengthy political legacy. He was named after his great-grandfather, a friend of George Washington's and one of the signers of the Declaration of Independence. Benjamin's grandfather, William Henry Harrison, was elected as president when Benjamin was seven years old.

Benjamin was tutored at home. He seemed to believe from the start that he was destined for greatness. Harrison graduated near the top of his class at Miami University in Ohio in 1852. He married his college sweetheart, Caroline Lavinia Scott, a year later. After studying law in Cincinnati, he passed the Ohio bar exam in 1854. Harrison moved to Indianapolis, Indiana, and practiced law there for eight years.

When the Republican Party produced its first presidential nominee, John C. Fremont, Harrison joined the party and campaigned for him. Harrison began his political career a year later as the Indianapolis city attorney.

Benjamin Harrison was the 23rd president of the United States. He was the grandson of William Henry Harrison, the 9th president of the United States.

Harrison joined the 70th Indiana Infantry Regiment in 1862. He was promoted from lieutenant to brigadier general before retiring in June 1865. Harrison served under Major General William T. Sherman. He was among the first to march into Atlanta, Georgia, when it surrendered to Union forces in 1864.

After the Civil War, Harrison returned to Indiana. He failed in an attempt to gain the Republican nomination for governor in 1872. He was nominated four years later but lost the election.

President Rutherford B. Hayes appointed Harrison to the Mississippi River Commission in 1879, beginning his career in national politics. Harrison served as a U.S. Senator from 1881 to 1887. A year after leaving the Senate, he spoke of rejuvenating the Republican Party while running for president. Harrison's campaign speeches, from a front porch in Indianapolis, were aimed at the press and selected delegations. Harrison supported pensions for Civil War veterans and a strong tariff to protect U.S. business interests. Although he lost the popular vote, winning New York helped Harrison comfortably win the electoral votes needed to become president.

Harrison fought in the Civil War on the Union side.

WILLIAM HENRY HARRISON

Benjamin's grandfather, William Henry Harrison, was elected as the ninth president. He died at the White House 32 days into his term.

Harrison, who was 68 when elected, was the second-oldest president to take office. Only Ronald Reagan was older. Harrison became ill after delivering his inaugural address. He died of a respiratory infection, believed to have been pneumonia. He was the first president to die while in office.

Harrison's Presidency and Legacy

Harrison began the process of making the United States stronger in international affairs. Harrison expanded the U.S. Navy, which allowed the United States to contend with Spain in the years to come. This helped to make the country into the military power it would become in the next century.

Harrison battled Chile, winning concessions and a formal apology for the mistreatment of American sailors in Valparaiso, Chile, where two sailors were killed and several injured in a fight outside a bar. He stood up to Great Britain and Canada on conservation issues, such as the protection of seals in the Bering Sea. Under his guidance, Samoa became an American **protectorate**, marking the first time the United States officially showed its strength by formally protecting a weaker state.

Harrison developed trade with key American markets. He organized the first modern Pan-American Conference in late 1889 to increase U.S. influence in Latin America. Harrison tried to get Congress behind a plan to build a canal in Nicaragua. Although this did not happen, the idea was the groundwork for the United States' involvement in the development of the Panama Canal.

The greatest expansion of the United States took place under Harrison's leadership, although much of it came at the expense of American Indians.

North Dakota, South Dakota, Montana, and Washington all became states in November 1889. Idaho and Wyoming obtained statehood in July

> "We Americans have a commission from God to police the world."
>
> *Benjamin Harrison*

Harrison and his administration were active in foreign affairs.

1890. The Sioux Indians lost more than 11 million acres in the Dakotas. Harrison released almost 2 million acres each from the Indian Territory of Oklahoma in late 1889 and from the Crow Indian reservation in Montana in 1892.

Harrison actively sought to expand foreign trade. Presidential powers of foreign trade were increased through the McKinley Tariff Act of 1890. The tariffs caused high prices and, along with the Sherman Silver Purchase Act, became a source of controversy as the country sunk into economic decline.

Following his presidency, Harrison remained informed in foreign affairs. He served as chief counsel for Venezuela in a border dispute with British Guiana. Harrison remarried after his first wife, Caroline, died in 1892. He died March 13, 1901, of pneumonia at his home in Indianapolis.

HAWAI'I CONTROVERSY

Benjamin Harrison sought to annex the Hawai'ian Islands during his presidency. He sent 150 marines to protect a government made up of settlers that overthrew the Hawai'ian Queen Liliuokalani. The settlers offered a treaty of annexation, but the Senate refused to grant Harrison's wishes.

U.S. pineapple and sugar corporations had strong interests in Hawai'i and had aided in the overthrow. It was not until 1898, five years after Harrison left office, that the U.S. annexed Hawai'i as a territory.

A Sioux Indian delegation went to Washington, D.C., in 1891 to gain government support for more food and better treatment for the Sioux people.

William McKinley's Early Years and Early Political Career

William McKinley was born January 29, 1843, in Niles, Ohio. He was the seventh child of William McKinley, Sr., and Nancy Allison McKinley. William Jr. developed a strong work ethic from his father, who owned a small iron foundry. He learned the value of courtesy and honesty from his devoutly religious mother.

The family moved to Poland, Ohio, when McKinley was 10 years old. There, he studied at a school which was run by the Methodist seminary. McKinley attended Allegheny College in Meadville, Pennsylvania, for one year before he became ill and financial problems forced him to return home.

McKinley joined the 23rd Ohio Volunteer Infantry at the start of the Civil War. McKinley was an officer under Colonel Rutherford B. Hayes, the future president, who became his mentor. The 19-year-old soldier was praised for his bravery in the Battle of Antietam. McKinley drove a wagon, pulled by mules, through the battlefield under Confederate fire in order to deliver food to weary troops.

McKinley earned many promotions throughout the Civil War. After the war, he retired as a major and returned home to begin a law career. He passed the bar exam in 1867 and practiced law in Canton, Ohio.

McKinley began as a county prosecutor in 1869 and rose through the Republican party. While beginning to work in politics, McKinley met his future wife, Ida Saxton. They were married in 1871. He ran successfully for Congress in 1876. McKinley held the position until 1891, with the exception of part of a

William McKinley was the 25th president of the United States.

two-year term when the House Committee on Elections overturned his apparent victory in 1882.

McKinley served on the House Ways and Means Committee, which worked on tax issues. He was a strong advocate of tariffs and presented the McKinley Tariff Act, a bill that was passed in 1890.

> **"That's all a man can hope for during his lifetime—to set an example—and when he is dead, to be an inspiration for history."** *President William McKinley*

McKinley's political career was thriving despite sadness at home. Both of his children died in the 1870s, one as an infant, and one as a 3-year-old. In the aftermath of the deaths of her children and her mother, Ida Saxton McKinley became ill and depressed. She never fully recovered, struggling with serious illness until her death in 1907. Ida's illness led to medical expenses, which made it difficult for the future president to pay his bills.

After falling short of a bid to become the Speaker of the House, McKinley returned to Ohio. He was elected governor in 1891 and 1893. He was credited with reforming Ohio's public schools and prisons and supporting factory workers.

William and Ida McKinley struggled with the loss of their children.

The Election of 1896 and McKinley's Presidency

> **"We need Hawai'i just as much and a good deal more than we did California. It is Manifest Destiny."**
> *William McKinley*

Economic difficulties stemming from the stock market crash in 1893 left the Democratic Party in a difficult position as the 1896 election approached. The Republicans, on the other hand, needed just one ballot to make it clear that McKinley would be their nominee for president.

The Republicans endorsed the backing of all money in gold, and McKinley continued backing strong tariffs. The Democrats nominated William Jennings Bryan and returned to the position of supporting **bimetallism**, which based money on both gold and silver.

The Populist Party, which had made itself a factor in the 1892 election by backing James B. Weaver and winning some farming states, backed the nomination of Bryan. The Populist Party believed in free silver coinage and a large amount of paper money. They believed in the abolishment of the National Bank. This coalition between the Populist and Democratic parties concerned the Republican Party. They used the support of big business and banking to raise a stunning $4 million in campaign contributions. Republicans distributed 200 million campaign pamphlets.

McKinley campaigned for president from the porch of his home in Canton, Ohio.

Bryan lost support from the members of the Democratic Party who believed in a gold standard. McKinley won with a sizeable amount of the popular vote and electoral votes going to him.

True to his positions before running for president, McKinley sought strong tariffs to continue the nation's economic recovery. Nelson R. Dingley, the chairman of the House Ways and Means Committee, sponsored the Dingley Tariff Act. The act again raised tariffs by 49 percent, but gave the president the power to negotiate reductions and items that could be duty-free. In 1896, the largest portion of the federal budget was the $160 million generated by customs duties.

The United States was upset over the treatment of Cubans who were rebelling against Spanish control. The United States had many business interests within Cuba, causing concern over the potential economic impact. McKinley was reluctant to consider military force early on, but when war was declared on Spain April 25, 1898, McKinley immediately pushed a resolution through Congress to annex the Hawai'ian Islands. Hawai'i secured U.S. Navy positions with its central location in the Pacific Ocean. The Spanish-American War included issues with territories in the Pacific Ocean, as well as the Caribbean Sea, making it an important time to resolve the issue involving Hawai'i.

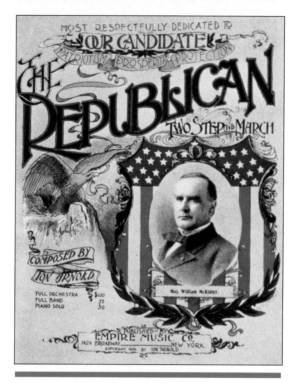

The Republican Two Step and March was a song composed in honor of McKinley.

U.S.S. *MAINE*

Spanish supporters protested negotiations with Cuban rebels in the Cuban capital of Havana in January 1898. To protect U.S. citizens and property in the increasingly tense situation, President William McKinley ordered the U.S.S. *Maine*, a battleship, to be positioned in Havana Harbor.

When the *Maine* sunk in Havana Harbor February 15, 1898, following an explosion, 266 Americans died. McKinley ordered an investigation into the explosion, but American sentiment at the time led to the assumption that Spain had to be involved in the explosion. A little more than two months later, the two nations were at war.

The Spanish-American War

Discontent among Spanish colonies in the Caribbean Sea and the Pacific Ocean led to the United States expanding its territorial control near the end of the 19th century.

> **"We want no wars of conquest; we must avoid the temptation of territorial aggression."**
> *William McKinley*

Conflict grew between the United States and Spain from 1895, until the brief war fought in 1898. Cuba had failed twice before in its quest for independence from Spain. In 1895, Cuba began a third battle. The United States pledged its support for Cuba.

Similar unrest grew in Puerto Rico, Guam, and the Philippines. Spain fought to defend its territory. The United States believed these nations should be free of Spanish rule. European powers, led by Germany, appealed for peace between the two countries. The explosion of the U.S.S. *Maine* intensified U.S. public opinion against Spain.

The United States publicly recognized Cuba's independence on April 19, 1898. Spain declared war on the United States on April 23. The United States declared war on Spain two days later.

Within a week, the U.S. Navy moved in on Manila Bay in the Philippines. The United States repeatedly overwhelmed Spain in naval battles. Land battles were limited. Theodore Roosevelt organized a First United States Volunteer Cavalry. He led a regiment known as the "Rough Riders" up Kettle Hill in San Juan Hill, Cuba, in the Spanish-American War's best-known battle.

The Treaty of Paris ended the war. As part of the treaty, the United

The U.S.S. *Maine* sank after an explosion in Havana Harbor, Cuba.

States acquired Guam, Puerto Rico, and the Philippines from Spain. They became territories of the United States. Spain was paid about $20 million for the Philippines. Cuba was declared independent, but remained under U.S. protection and influence until 1934.

The United States annexed Hawai'i in 1898, creating protection for the western part of the country through a strategic naval base. Following the Spanish-American War, the people of the Philippines fought U.S. occupation. They remained a U.S. territory until they were granted independence in 1946. Puerto Rico is still a self-governing commonwealth of the United States.

Theodore Roosevelt led a group of men called the "Rough Riders" who fought in the Spanish-American War. Roosevelt became president in 1901.

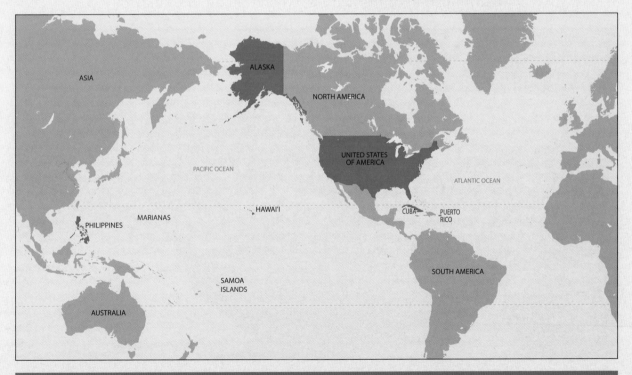

This map shows in red the territories and possessions of the United States in 1899.

McKinley's Assassination and Legacy

The United States became involved in more matters beyond its borders. After dealing with issues in the Caribbean Sea and Pacific Ocean during the Spanish-American War, the next foreign policy concerned trade with China. Japanese and European interests had expanded their influence over China in the 1890s. The United States feared that Chinese ports might be closed to trade with the United States. McKinley worked with Secretary of State John Hay on the "Open Door" policy. This policy stated that the United States wanted all nations to be on equal footing, without discrimination or restrictions, when trading in China.

> "The American people, entrenched in freedom, take their love for it wherever they go."
> *William McKinley*

U.S. troops crossed a river to attack a Chinese arsenal in the Boxer Rebellion.

In 1898, the Boxers, a group of Chinese nationalists protesting foreign intrusion in their country, massacred missionaries and attacked diplomats in Peking. In 1900, McKinley sent gunboats and 2,500 troops to assist multi-national forces in freeing the diplomats. McKinley and Hay made it clear that the United States was supporting action to free the diplomats, not to assist Japan or European nations in taking control of China. The Allied forces put down the Boxer Rebellion, forcing China to pay millions of dollars in damages to each country.

The economy was improving, and McKinley had led the United States into position as a world power. War hero Theodore Roosevelt, the governor of New York, was added as the vice presidential candidate in the 1900 election. In a rematch with Bryan, McKinley won with an even larger margin of popular votes.

McKinley remained an active president, traveling often. Early in his second term, McKinley was in Buffalo, New York, to speak at the Pan-American Exposition. On the afternoon of September 6, 1901, McKinley shook hands with the crowd at a public reception at the exposition's Temple of Music. McKinley reached to shake the hand of Leon Czolgosz, who fired a shot from a concealed revolver into the president's chest.

While his wounds were being treated, McKinley urged his guards not to hurt Czolgosz, a 28-year-old, unemployed Detroit millworker. He told his private secretary to break the news gently to his wife. There was a chance that McKinley might be able to recover from the wounds but gangrene, tissue death caused by infection or loss of blood supply, set in around the wound. President McKinley died September 14, 1901. Czolgosz, who called the president an enemy of the working people, was executed by electric chair on October 29, 1901.

McKinley left the presidency in the hands of Roosevelt. McKinley also left the Republican Party in a position of power. His decisive victories led to an era in which Woodrow Wilson was the only non-Republican to occupy the White House through 1932.

Leon Czolgosz was sent to prison before being executed on October 29, 1901.

Timeline

The development of the industrial United States from 1870 to 1900 took the country from rebuilding after the Civil War to becoming a world power in many ways. The United States began to export more products than ever before. The foreign policy of the presidents in this era led to the expansion of the United States, gaining territories in the Caribbean Sea and Pacific Ocean. During the Spanish-American

1870-1874	1875-1879	1880-1884

PRESIDENTS

Chester Arthur is appointed Collector of the Port of New York in 1871.

Samuel J. Tilden wins the popular vote, but Rutherford B. Hayes takes the disputed 1876 election by one electoral vote.

James A. Garfield is shot by an assassin just months after taking office in 1881. He dies later in the year.

UNITED STATES

The 15th Amendment to the Constitution is ratified in 1870, giving African-American men the right to vote.

The United States celebrates its centennial with the first World's Fair in Philadelphia, Pennsylvania, on July 4, 1876.

Clara Barton founds the American Association of the Red Cross in 1881.

WORLD

Italy is unified in 1870 after troops seize Rome from French forces.

In 1877, Great Britain expands its empire when it annexes the South African Republic and Queen Victoria is proclaimed empress of India.

Volcano Krakatoa erupts in 1883, wiping out 136 Indonesian villages and killing more than 36,000 people.

War, the United States had shown the world that it could contend with European powers. At home, the presidents in this era fought patronage and corruption to make sure its leaders were chosen for their expertise and not their connections. This era was also a troubled time. Labor unions battled companies for fair wages. The stock market crash of 1893 led to a nation-wide economic depression. Two presidents were assassinated within 20 years. Through the hardship and the prosperity of the industrial era, the United States emerged as a modern nation.

1885-1889	1890-1894	1895-1900

PRESIDENTS

| Benjamin Harrison, the grandson of president William Henry Harrison, takes office in 1889. | Grover Cleveland, who served as president from 1885 to 1889, returns for a second term in 1893.  | William McKinley wins the 1896 election. |

UNITED STATES

| The Statue of Liberty is unveiled in New York October 28, 1886.  | The stock market crashes June 27, 1893, contributing to a depression. | Hawai'i is annexed as a U.S. territory in 1898.  |

WORLD

| Louis Pasteur administers the first anti-rabies vaccine in 1885.  | In 1893, New Zealand grants female suffrage, making it the first country to allow women to vote in national elections. | Control over Guam, Puerto Rico, and the Philippines is transferred from Spain to the United States following the Spanish-American War in 1898. |

Activity

Taxes are a necessity to run a government. They are used for everything from helping to pay elected officials to covering the cost of building roads.

Over a period of time, like a week, make a list of what items are taxed and at what amount. Many receipts will show the amount of tax paid. What is taxed at the store? At a restaurant? At a gas station? You may need to look at a sign on a gas pump to determine the amount.

Talk to a parent, teacher, or other adult. Ask them for other examples of ways they pay taxes. Do they know the percent of taxes added to certain bills?

With a calculator, you can determine the percentage of tax on an item. For example, if there is $1.21 in taxes added to a bill for $20.17 of groceries, you can divide 1.21 by 20.17, which comes out to 0.0599. This rounds to 0.06. Percent means "per one hundred," so 0.06 is 6 percent. Make sure you use the amount before taxes when calculating.

Once you have a list of taxed items, compare the percentages. Are all items taxed the same? Is there a reason for them to be taxed differently? Does this seem fair?

Based on what you have read in this book, do you think items could be taxed differently depending on where they were made and other factors?

Would all candidates for president have the same beliefs on this subject?

Think about what you might believe would be a fair way to tax items if you were going to run for president either now or in an era of a developing nation, such as the United States from 1870 to 1900.

Quiz

1. Which president did not fight in the Civil War?
   A. Rutherford B. Hayes
   B. James Garfield
   C. Grover Cleveland

2. Labor Day came about in the aftermath of which event?
   A. Bland-Allison Act
   B. Pullman Strike
   C. Spanish-American War

3. Which country gained independence after the Spanish-American War?
   A. Cuba
   B. Puerto Rico
   C. Guam

4. Prohibition outlawed the use of which product?
   A. tobacco
   B. alcohol
   C. coffee

5. Which two presidents were assassinated during the industrial era?
   A. Rutherford B. Hayes and Grover Cleveland
   B. Rutherford B. Hayes and Benjamin Harrison
   C. James Garfield and William McKinley

6. True or False? Pullman workers went on strike because their wages increased but their housing costs also increased.

7. True or False? Hawai'i became a state in 1898.

8. True or False? Belva Lockwood was the first woman to practice law in front of the Supreme Court.

9. True or False? Rutherford B. Hayes is the only person to serve two non-consecutive terms as president.

Answers 1. C 2. B 3. A 4. B 5. C 6. False. Their wages decreased while their housing costs stayed the same. 7. False. Hawai'i became a U.S. territory in 1898. It did not become a state until 1959. 8. True 9. False. Grover Cleveland is the only president to serve two non-consecutive terms.

Further Research

Books

To find out more about United States presidents, visit your local library. Most libraries have computers that connect to a database for researching information. If you input a key word, you will be provided with a list of books in the library that contain information on that topic. Non-fiction books are arranged numerically, using their call number. Fiction books are organized alphabetically by the author's last name.

Websites

The World Wide Web is a good source of information. Reputable websites include government sites, educational sites, and online encyclopedias. Visit the following sites to learn more about U.S. presidents.

The official White House website offers a short history of the U.S. presidency, along with biographical sketches and portraits of all the presidents to date. **www.whitehouse.gov/history/presidents**

This website contains background information, election results, cabinet members, and notable events for each of the presidents. **www.ipl.org/div/potus**

Explore the lives and careers of every U.S. president on the PBS website. **www.pbs.org/wgbh/amex/presidents**

Glossary

abolitionist: a person who believes in the elimination of slavery

bimetallism: the belief in a money system based on both gold and silver

economic depression: a period in which business, employment, and stock-market values decline severely or remain at a low level

electoral college: electors chosen to represent the popular vote in each state in voting for the president of the United States

export: to ship goods out of a country

greenbacks: paper money that was not backed by gold

import: to ship goods into a country

nominee: a politician who a party names to run for office

patronage: distributing political jobs and favors based on connections, not expertise

prohibition: the legal ban on the manufacture and sale of alcohol

protectorate: protection and partial control by a more powerful country over a dependent country or region

ratified: signed or given formal consent

suffrage: the right to vote

tariffs: taxes charged on imports or exports

temperance: restraint from the use of alcohol

veto: the right of a president to reject bills passed by Congress

Index